DATE DUE

War in the Gulf

THE ARMED FORCES

Written By: Bob Italia

Published by Abdo & Daughters, 6535 Cecilia Circle, Edina, Minnesota 55439.

Library bound edition distributed by Rockbottom Books, Pentagon Tower, P.O. Box 36036, Minneapolis, Minnesota 55435.

Library of Congress Number: 91-073075   ISBN: 1-56239-026-0

Cover Photo by: Bettmann
Inside Photos by: Reuters/Bettmann
                  UPI/Bettmann: 44

Edited by: Rosemary Wallner

TABLE OF CONTENTS

American Forces digging in along the Kuwait/Saudi Arabia border.

FOUR BRANCHES, ONE FORCE

On August 2, 1990, Iraqi military forces invaded the tiny country of Kuwait. By August 7, 160,000 Iraqi troops massed on Saudi Arabia's border. It looked as though Saudi Arabia would be next.

Fearing invasion, Saudi Arabia requested military help from the United States. On August 8, 1990, the Rapid Deployment Forces of the United States Army and Air Force were on their way to Saudi Arabia — the beginning of "Operation Desert Shield."

While American forces dug in along the Kuwait/Saudi Arabia border, the United Nations authorized the use of force if Iraq did not leave Kuwait by January 15, 1991. The deadline came and went. Iraq refused to withdraw from Kuwait.

On January 16, 1991, "Operation Desert Shield" became "Operation Desert Storm" when America and its allies launched a massive air strike against Iraqi forces.

Operation Desert Storm (January 16 - February 27, 1991) was the most massive display of military power since the Vietnam War. It employed hundreds of thousands of military personnel from all four branches of the U.S. Armed Forces, and an amazing array of high-tech military weapons and equipment.

What were the roles of each branch of the U.S. Armed Forces during the Gulf War? How did they work together to earn such an incredible victory over Iraq? These are some of the questions that will be answered in this book.

Marine fighter jets line the flight deck of the USS Independence.

THE MARINES
SPEARHEADING THE INVASION

The United States Marine Corps officially began in 1798 as part of the Navy. Today it remains part of the Navy with nearly 200,000 active personnel, and 90,000 reserves.

The Marines also have their own armored equipment and aircraft, including 700 tanks, 400 infantry fighting vehicles, 800 armored personnel carriers, 1000 pieces of artillery, 80 helicopters, and 490 combat aircraft.

The Marines conduct ground operations in connection with naval operations, usually beginning with an amphibious landing launched from Navy ships. (The marines have equipment that can be used in water and on land). Typically, it is the Marines who will begin a ground war on enemy territory by storming enemy shores and beaches.

The Marines first fought in the War of 1812. But they didn't establish themselves as an important branch of the U.S. military until World War II.

It was the Marines who recaptured many Pacific islands taken by Japanese forces during this war, including Iwo Jima and the Philippines.

U.S. Marines of the 1st Division training along the Kuwait/Saudi Arabia border.

Operation Desert Storm

The Marines of the 1st Division were the first U.S. troops to fight the Iraqi army. That was their task. It happened in mid-January 1991 when Operation Desert Storm was first launched.

The Marines of the 1st Division had been in position along the Kuwaiti border since August 1990. The Iraqis shelled the Marine positions with artillery fire and missiles. Marine scouts spotted the Iraqi artillery positions and called in their deadly Cobra helicopter gunships and A-10 Thunderbolts.

"We just ran up on it (Iraqi artillery) and hit it with TOW rockets and 20mm cannon fire," said one of the Cobra pilots. "We were getting a little return fire from small arms and what may have been an antitank missile. There was just a flash and something zipped past.

"We continued to fire on it for five minutes," he added. "We used several TOWs, rockets and gunfire to make sure we took out anybody else who was hanging around the area. While it was first happening, we were concentrating on the attack, so it wasn't terribly frightening. But it did make me more apprehensive about running in on the next target."

The Marines were also used to capture oil platforms off the shores of Kuwait. These platforms were being used by the Iraqis as antiaircraft gun and missile sites.

In one battle, which shows how the Navy and the Marines work together, the *USS Nichols*, a guided missile frigate, attacked two Iraqi gunboats, sinking one. Then the *Nichols* approached one of the offshore oil platforms so the Marines could capture it.

Gunfire erupted immediately. The Marines returned the fire with rifles and machine guns. The battle was slow but intense as bullets streaked through the air. Three hours later, the platform was captured. Marine medics gave first aid to five wounded Iraqis while Marine guards kept watch over the newly captured prisoners.

A Marine was also the first to receive a Purple Heart (a medal given for being wounded in action). Medic Clerence Conner, 19, was part of a Marine patrol that came under intense artillery fire.

A shell exploded close to Conner, and a fiery piece of shrapnel tore into his shoulder.

Conner was evacuated to a desert hospital tent where his wound was treated. Normally, when a soldier receives a bad wound such as Conner's, he is eventually sent home. But Conner, displaying a typical Marine pride, asked to be returned to duty.

Marine aircraft also played an important role in Operation Desert Storm. Marine Harriers based in Saudi Arabia were sent in to Kuwait to destroy an Iraqi radio communication center. The Marine Harriers swept in fast and low and dropped 500-pound demolition bombs and cluster bombs.

"We obliterated it," said one of the Marine pilots. "We got the radio post and some other buildings."

Marine aircraft also attacked elsewhere. "My planes subjected the Iraqi Republican Guard to constant, continual bombing with no letup," said a Marine colonel. It was this constant bombing that led to the rout of the Iraqi army.

The Marine 1st and 2nd Divisions were also combined with the Army's heavy armored brigade along the Kuwaiti border for the big push into Kuwait. Using the M1A1 Abrams tanks and

Bradley Fighting Vehicles, the Marines skirted the deadly Iraqi minefields and fortified bunkers and pushed their way to the outskirts of Kuwait City. They encountered little resistance from the Iraqis, most of whom eagerly surrendered before any shots were fired.

The Marines also had a unique role in Operation Desert Storm. They were used as decoys. Since Iraq knew that the Marines were usually the first to launch a strike, they kept a good number of troops in place along the eastern shores of Kuwait where the Marines, aboard Navy ships, were stationed. By the time the coalition forces swept into Kuwait from the south and west, it was too late for the Iraqi forces along the coast to repel the attack.

Scout Snipers — An Elite Marine Unit

Marine Scout Snipers are dressed in camouflage suits that are so deceiving, you can walk by them and never see them. They carry M40A1s, special high-powered rifles with equally powerful scopes that allow them to kill from a thousand yards away. Their mission is to eliminate selected targets such as enemy scouts, and find the most secure route of travel for friendly troops.

U.S. soldiers from the 1st Armoured Division heading to the front in their Bradley Fighting Vehicle.

THE NAVY
FIRING THE FIRST SHOT

The U.S. Navy officially came into existence in 1798. It now consists of nearly 600,000 active personnel with reserves of nearly 250,000. Its major divisions include the Sixth Fleet in the Mediterranean Sea, the Second Fleet in the North Atlantic, the Third Fleet off the U.S. Pacific coast, and the Seventh Fleet in the Western Pacific.

The Navy operates four battleships, 41 cruisers, 68 destroyers, 66 amphibious warfare ships, 93 nuclear attack submarines, 35 ballistic missile submarines, 14 aircraft carriers, 152 support ships, and 1,580 of its own aircraft.

The Navy saw its first action in the early 19th century during the Barbary Coast wars. It played a major role in World War I and II by helping spread America's military might around the world. The war against Japan could not have been won without the Navy. Today, the Navy remains one of the most important branches of the U.S. Armed Forces, giving America a powerful military presence worldwide.

U.S. Defense Secretary Richard Cheney (right) talks to U.S. Navy servicemen.

Operation Desert Storm

The Navy's task in Operation Desert Storm was to obtain control of the Persian Gulf, protect friendly ships, stop Iraqi trade, and launch an attack against Iraq. Much of the heavy armor, supplies, and troops of Operation Desert Shield and Desert Storm were transported to the Middle East by the Navy.

Navy ships stationed in the Persian Gulf prevented supplies from being shipped to Iraq during Operation Desert Shield. The first shot fired in Operation Desert Storm was from a Navy ship — in the form of a Tomahawk cruise missile.

The powerful battleships *Wisconsin* and *Missouri* were the most talked about Navy ships. By the end of the first week of Operation Desert Storm, these two ships had fired nearly 200 Tomahawk cruise missiles at Iraq — most of which struck with deadly accuracy at Baghdad, Iraq's capital, which was over 100 miles away.

"I wouldn't want to be anywhere else in the Navy," said one member of a Tomahawk firing team. "I enjoyed hearing those live news broadcasts from Baghdad.

I understand they heard bombs exploding all over the place, but couldn't hear any planes. That's because there *were* no planes!"

The big guns on the battleships also softened Iraqi positions in Kuwait, paving the way for the ground assault. Navy and Marine pilots flew thousands of "sorties" (missions) and accounted for nearly 40 percent of all missions flown.

Other than launching cruise missiles, shelling Iraqi positions, and launching aircraft, the Navy had little else to do in the way of fighting. That's because the Iraqi navy and air force refused to engage the U.S. Navy in battle, fearing its lethal firepower. Occasionally, the Navy encountered an Iraqi gunboat. The gunboats were sunk before they could get close enough to fire a shot. The Navy also used their minesweepers to help clear the Persian Gulf of powerful Iraqi mines. Navy hospital ships were stationed in the Persian Gulf in the event that the war turned bloody. But fortunately for the coalition forces, these ships weren't necessary.

The Navy Seals

The Navy Seals are the most famous Navy commandos. It is their job to pave the way for amphibious assaults on enemy shores and beaches.

In Operation Desert Storm, Navy Seals swam to Kuwaiti beaches and removed underwater mines. They also cut fiber-optic cables that Iraqi commanders used to communicate with their troops, used laser beams to pinpoint bombing targets, and obtained soil samples to find the best invasion routes.

Without such special assistance from these commandos, Operation Desert Storm would not have been the incredible success story that it became.

THE ARMY
THE THUNDER AND LIGHTNING OF DESERT STORM

The U.S. Army is the ground service of the Armed Forces. Officially established in 1785, the Army has nearly 800,000 personnel. It has 18 active divisions, 10 National Guard divisions, and 12 reserve divisions.

The Army is equipped with most of the heavy armor and artillery in the U.S. arsenal. It has 16,000 tanks, 2,250 helicopters, 5,000 infantry fighting vehicles, 26,000 armored personnel carriers, and 5,400 pieces of artillery.

The U.S. Army first saw action in the War of 1812. One of its brightest moments came during World War II when it helped push the German Army from France. Today, the Army remains the backbone of America's armed forces.

U.S. Army maintained land control with their mechanized fighting power.

Operation Desert Storm

The Army's task in Operation Desert Storm was to defend Saudi Arabia and win the ground war against Iraq. Without the U.S. Army, Operation Desert Storm would not have been able to push the Iraqi forces from Kuwait. Their awesome collection of firepower and the speed with which they struck made it impossible for Iraqi troops to maintain control of the land. Most of Iraq's army fled at the terrible sight of the rumbling, mechanized U.S. Army. Those who stayed and fought either surrendered or died.

The Iraqi military had never seen anything like it. After relentless pounding by its heavy artillery, the U.S. Army launched its attack at night, adding to the confusion and terror.

Spearheading the attack were thousands of M1A1 Abrams main battle tanks. They roared over, around, and through Iraqi fortifications at speeds of 40 miles per hour firing their deadly 120mm guns with incredible accuracy. Then came wave after wave of mechanized infantry in their Bradley Fighting Vehicles.

Overhead, Army Cobra and Apache attack helicopters let loose a firestorm of Hellfire missiles and cannon fire, destroying Iraqi tanks, trucks, and artillery.

The U.S. Army attack was relentless. The Iraqis were overwhelmed. Those who survived were picked up by the follow-up forces while the mechanized U.S. forces rumbled on.

While the U.S. Army's heavy armor rolled over the Iraqi front lines, thousands of Army paratroopers descended on Iraqi airfields to seize control of them. Once on the ground, these paratroopers directed huge C-130 Hercules transports onto the safe stretches of cratered runways. More Army troops and heavy equipment poured out of the transports. Their job was to block the escape routes of the retreating Iraqi Army. Thousands of Iraqi troops were captured, loaded into transport trucks, then sent south to prisoner-of-war camps in Saudi Arabia. In four days, the ground war was over. The U.S. Army had done its job.

U.S. Army's heavy armor rolled over the Iraqi front.

Life in the Desert

Yes, the desert is hot and dry. But it can also be wet and cold.

As the members of the army infantry found out, the desert can get a lot of rain in a short amount of time. It rained four inches during one storm. The desert turned into a lake, and the troops had to wait until the sand slowly soaked up the water. Then the sand remained soft — too soft for the heavy tanks and equipment to travel through. It got cold at night, too. Often, the temperature dropped below freezing.

Dust was also a problem, but not as serious as first feared. Proper maintenance of all equipment was emphasized to keep the mechanized army rolling. Dust was the biggest problem to helicopter pilots whose rotating blades stirred the sand into mini-dust storms, making it difficult to land. Fortunately, no major accidents occurred because of the sand.

Home for most Army personnel was in a tent or bunker. Those near the front line were not so fortunate. They lived in their tanks or trucks — or sometimes in hastily dug foxholes. They slept in parka linings with socks on their hands. There were no hot showers, no beds, and the food ("Meals Ready to Eat" or "MRE rations") was plain, simple — and cold. Many troops hated the MREs except the starving Iraqi prisoners of war.

Open fires were not allowed on the front lines. Fires could reveal troop locations to the enemy. Hot coffee was available, but it had to be heated from tiny butane heaters that were kept in cardboard boxes. Swapping also became an everyday event: gloves for cigarettes, long underwear for candy, etc..

It was easy to get lost in the desert. There were no trees or bushes or much of anything else that marked the land. At night, it got even worse.

During Operation Desert Shield, the troops had a lot of free time as they waited for the ground war to start. They listened to music and news broadcast from four military FM stations called Desert Shield Radio. They read letters from home (tons of mail was received daily). Some played volleyball, baseball, and football. Others just sat . . . and waited for war.

There were many reasons the soldiers in the desert wanted the war to end quickly. Leaving behind life in the desert was one of the greatest.

U.S. Marines keep their guns close by even when showering.

U.S. Marines play volleyball to relieve themselves from the boredom during Operation Desert Shield.

Spec Ops Commandos

The Army's Special Operations (Spec Ops) commandos such as the famed Rangers, Delta Force, and Green Berets played a very secret — but important part in the war. Long before Operation Desert Storm was launched, these commandos had already gone into action.

One secret mission happened in December 1990. Flying at night in Soviet MI-8 Hip helicopters painted in Iraqi camouflage colors, the Army commandos were sent deep into Iraq to capture a Soviet-made SA-8 surface-to-air missile (SAM). The Army wanted to examine the missile because it had a new radar-guidance system.

"It was a brilliant operation," said a Pentagon official. "Those guys flew in, took the Iraqis completely by surprise, interrogated the crew, took the missile and flew back." The commandos also captured Iraqi combat plans. When Operation Desert Storm was launched, the U.S. knew how these SAM missiles worked, and what plans the Iraqis had made to fight the coalition forces.

Another operation was carried out by the Green Berets and Delta Force commandos wearing night vision goggles. They parachuted into enemy territory with camouflaged motorcycles and dune buggies equipped with motor-silencing mufflers. Then the commandos roamed the desert looking for mobile Scud missile launchers. Once located, the missile launcher positions were relayed to a satellite from hand-held transmitters. Minutes later, F-15 bombers swept in and destroyed the launchers.

PsyOps

Psychological Warfare Units (PsyOps) are also part of the Army. They are responsible for weakening the enemy's will to fight.

In one such operation, thousands of portable radios, VCR tapes, and audio cassettes were smuggled into Kuwait and Iraq. The radios and audio tapes broadcast news and messages about the pounding the Iraqis were taking — and the VCR tapes showed it! This made many of the Iraqi soldiers fearful of the war.

There are many other ways PsyOps are used against an enemy. Most of this information is classified top-secret.

Patriot Control Unit

Patriot missiles did very well against the Iraqi Scuds. Most of the Scuds were destroyed before they could strike their targets. But without the specially-trained Army control units that operate the high-tech antimissile system, the Scuds would have gotten through.

The soldiers at the control unit have little time to react once an enemy missile appears on the radar screen.

"I knew right away what it was," said a control unit officer stationed at a Patriot site in Saudi Arabia. "There's no way you can confuse it."

A Scud was on its way. Time to launch a Patriot.

"It was like a big, brilliant flare," the officer said of the launching. "It jumped off the ground, snaked back and forth a few times — and then BOOM!" The Scud came to earth in a shower of flaming debris.

Having high-tech weapons systems is one thing. Having the right people operating them can spell the difference between life and death.

THE AIR FORCE
WINNING THE WAR BEFORE IT STARTS

The U.S. Air Force began as the Aeronautical Division of the Army in 1907. During World War II, it was still considered part of the Army. But in 1947, under the Department of Defense's National Security Act, the Air Force became its own branch of America's Armed Forces.

The Air Force has an active force of nearly 600,000 men and women. About 130,000 are in reserve. There is also an Air National Guard of 115,000. The Air Force has 3,200 combat aircraft, 360 bombers, and 1,000 Intercontinental Ballistic Missiles (ICBMs).

The Air Force was a minor presence in World War I. "Dogfights" between enemy and friendly aircraft received much attention, but the bulk of the war was fought on land and at sea.

During World War II, however, the role of the Air Force began to change. Aircraft made it possible to launch bombing raids around the world. Aircraft carriers could hold many planes. They could position themselves in oceans around the world, and the destructive power of their aircraft became very great. In the war against Germany, U.S. and Allied bombers destroyed Germany's industrial might, making it impossible for the Germans to continue waging war. In the war against Japan, two U.S. Flying Fortresses dropped the first atomic bombs — which ended World War II.

Today, the U.S. Air Force is one of the most powerful military forces in the world. It can strike anywhere and at anytime with a destructive force greater than all the world wars put together.

The Stealth fighter waits to be armed for a bombing run in Iraq.

Operation Desert Storm

The Air Force's task in Operation Desert Storm was to obtain air superiority, provide air support for the ground troops, strike enemy targets in Kuwait and Iraq, and airlift Army and Marine forces. When Operation Desert Storm was launched, it was the Air Force that conducted most of the strikes against the Iraqi military.

From air bases in Saudi Arabia, Turkey, England, Egypt, and the tiny island of Diego Garcia in the Indian Ocean, wave after wave of fighter bombers, fighter planes, and strategic bombers pounded Iraqi military positions in Kuwait and Iraq.

Many experts believe that the air strikes were responsible for the quick four-day ground war. Seeing the destruction wrought by the Air Force's conventional bombs, smart bombs and guided missiles, it's hard to disagree with them.

B-52s pounded Iraqi's army day and night. By the time the ground war started, most of these troops were ready to surrender.

F-15s, F-16s, F-111s, Harriers, A-10 Warthogs, and an assortment of other terrifying machines destroyed Iraq's communication centers, bridges, power plants, chemical plants, munitions plants as well as thousands of tanks and artillery pieces with a precision never seen before. It marked the first time in military history that an air force had defeated an enemy before a ground war was launched.

U.S. fighter pilot sits in the high-tech cockpit of his F-16, waiting to depart on a bombing mission in Iraq.

War Stories From the Cockpit

"We crossed the border high with our escort a couple of miles behind us," said an F-15 pilot. "I could see the outlines of Baghdad, lit up like a huge Christmas tree. The entire city was just sparkling at us."

Then the F-15 pilot came upon an Iraqi Mirage fighter — one of the few Iraqi aircraft that challenged the U.S. Air Force.

"My number three (a fellow F-15) had just turned south, and I was headed northeast on a different pattern," the pilot continued. "I don't know if the bogey (enemy plane) was chasing him, but I locked him up, confirmed he was a hostile and fired a missile."

The F-15 was twelve miles from the Mirage when it fired a Sparrow missile. It took the Sparrow a few seconds to strike its target.

"When the plane blew," said the pilot, "the whole sky lit up. It continued to burn all the way to the ground and then just blew up into a thousand pieces. It was pretty exciting."

So how did the pilot feel about shooting down an enemy aircraft?

"You're so busy, you don't have time for feelings,"
he said. "But once I got back to base, I felt good. I
never experienced this before. It's unfortunate
that we've had to go to war, but I guess there was
no other way."

F-15 fighter jet on the runway after completing a bombing mission over Iraq.

Another pilot — one of the first to attack Baghdad — described what he saw:

"I saw one of the most fantastic fireworks demonstrations ever — just like the Fourth of July," he said. "What a doozey to go up the first time. There's a lot more stuff up there than I thought there would be. The noise of the enemy fire was like a freight train."

Though the enemy fire looked impressive — especially on television — it did not work well. Most of the time, the Iraqis fired blindly into the sky — often after U.S. Air Force fighters had swooped past with their deadly cargo of bombs and missiles.

Iraq had surface-to-air missiles to defend Baghdad, but the Air Force's F-4G Wild Weasels protected U.S. aircraft from the missiles. The Wild Weasels come equipped with Electronic Counter-Measure equipment (ECM) that jam enemy radar. They also carry radar-seeking HARM missiles that destroy enemy radar-guided missiles.

None of the incredible successes the Air Force enjoyed would have been possible had it not been for years of training.

"The lesson learned from the raids was that the type of training we've been doing has really paid off," said one pilot. "Once we got up there, it was just like another day in the office. We did exactly what we've been training for years and years to do."

And they did it with devastating results never before seen on the battlefield.

Aerial view of the devastation in Iraq.

WOMEN IN BATTLE

Operation Desert Storm marked the first time in U.S. military history that women appeared on the front lines. Most women in the military still hold traditional roles such as cooks, clerks and nurses. But there were women in Operation Desert Shield and Desert Storm who were armorers, firefighters, strategic planners, and intelligence officers — many of whom served near the front line.

The female soldiers had their own tents and latrines. Still, there was not much privacy or comfort. They ate the same food as the men, and the gear they carried was just as heavy, and just like the men, the women had to dig foxholes in the sand. In the military, everyone digs.

A female U.S. Air Force soldier uses a hoist while unloading a C-5 transport aircraft.

THE MILITARY LEADERS OF OPERATION DESERT STORM

General Colin Powell

Four-star General Colin Powell is the chairman of the Joint Chiefs of Staff. This means he is the commander of all branches of the U.S. Armed Forces. He is the first African American to become the chairman of the Joint Chiefs of Staff. He is also the youngest man ever to hold that position.

The 53-year-old Powell is the son of Jamaican immigrants. He grew up in New York. He attended New York's City College where he was an average student. In college, Powell joined the Army Reserves.

Powell fought in the Vietnam War. He earned a Purple Heart after stepping on a mine, and a Soldier's Medal for pulling two fellow soldiers out of a burning helicopter.

Powell remained in active duty for fourteen years. Then, in 1972, he was named to a White House budget staff. He remained in the White House as an aide until 1987 when President Ronald Reagan appointed him as national security advisor.

Gen. Colin Powell, chairman of the Joint Chiefs of Staff.

Having completed his duties successfully, Powell was appointed chairman of the Joint Chiefs of Staff by President George Bush in 1989. When Iraq invaded Kuwait in 1990, Colin Powell became the head of Operation Desert Shield and Desert Storm.

Powell insisted that, if America went to war against Iraq, all forces should be put to use. He also insisted that the first strike be quick and massive. From the moment Operation Desert Storm was launched, it was obvious that Powell got his wish.

The success of Operation Desert Storm had made Colin Powell a national hero. There is talk that he may run for vice president — or even president. Others want to make him a five-star general.

If Colin Powell wants to run for political office, he's not saying. He has more important things on his mind: bringing the troops home, maintaining peace in the Middle East, and keeping America's military ready for action.

General H. Norman Schwarzkopf

Norman Schwarzkopf was the commander of all U.S. Forces in the Persian Gulf. The 56-year-old, four-star general got the nickname "Stormin' Norman" because of his forceful military approach. He is also called "The Bear" because of his 6-foot 3-inch, 240-pound frame.

A graduate of West Point Military Academy, Schwarzkopf was a military advisor to the Vietnamese Airborne in 1965. He returned to Vietnam in 1970 as a lieutenant colonel and commanded an infantry battalion. He came home from that war like most did, his confidence shattered — even though he won two Purple Hearts and three Silver Stars. Still, he refused to quit his military career. He knew that someday the military would regain its former glory.

When Iraq invaded Kuwait, Schwarzkopf suddenly had the chance he had been waiting for.

Schwarzkopf helped put together the battle plan for Operation Desert Storm. Most importantly, Schwarzkopf was also in charge of keeping all the branches of the military together in one effective fighting force — a task he completed flawlessly.

Nearly every day of the war, people around the world listened as the general gave his down-to-earth and upbeat reports on radio and television. He became almost as famous as President Bush. When the war ended, Schwarzkopf was called a hero for his careful and expert handling of the war.

Schwarzkopf plans to retire from the military. Congress is talking about giving him a fifth silver star, which is very rare. He doesn't know what he'll do once he retires. Some people want him to run for the Senate. Others think he should run for political office.

What does the General think of all this?

"The first night (home), after I spend time with my family, I'll open the Christmas presents they saved for me," he said. "Then Bear (his dog) and I will probably go for a long walk on the beach, and we'll mutually decide where we're going to from there."

Whatever he does, Norman Schwarzkopf will be a great success — just as he was as Commander of all U.S. Armed Forces in Operation Desert Storm.

GLOSSARY

ALLIED - Military forces from different countries united in a common cause.

AMPHIBIOUS - Can be used on land and in water.

ARSENAL - A stock of weapons and ammunition.

ARTILLERY - Large firing weapons such as cannons and missile launchers that are operated by crews.

BALLISTIC MISSILE - A long-range missile that falls freely from the air (not guided).

COALITION FORCES - The combined military forces of the United Nations.

COMMANDOS - A small fighting force trained for special, quick-strike missions.

DOGFIGHTS - A aerial battle between fighter planes.

FOXHOLES - A shallow pit dug by a soldier for protection against enemy fire.

FRIGATE - A swift, medium-sized warship that acts as a protective escort to aircraft carriers.

RESERVES - An inactive fighting force that can be called up to active duty in case of a military emergency.